# Herzog &
# de Meuron

THIS IS A CARLTON BOOK

Text and Design copyright © 2002 Carlton Publishing Group

Photographs copyright©Margherita Spiluttini

This edition published by Carlton Publishing Group 2002
20 Mortimer Street
London
W1T 3JW

A CIP catalogue for this book is available from the British Library.

ISBN 1 84222 674 6

Executive Editor: Sarah Larter
Design: Adam Wright/Mercer Design
Picture research: Claire Gouldstone
Production: Lisa French

Printed in Dubai

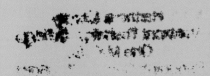

# Herzog &
# de Meuron

NAOMI STUNGO

CARLTON
BOOKS

On a sparkling winter morning late in 2001, the Swiss architect Jacques Herzog tucked the trouser legs of his immaculately tailored dark blue suit into a pair of somewhat too large Wellington boots, covered his long, closely shaven head with a hard hat and strode onto a muddy building site in the depths of one of London's poorer neighbourhoods to show a group of expectant journalists around what, even before it was finished, critics were confidently proclaiming one of the more astonishing modern buildings in Britain.

And no wonder. Even at this early stage the main elements of the dance school were all clearly visible: the great sweeping arc of the front façade, the corkscrew spiral staircases and ramps leading up from ground- to first-floor level, the shafts open to the elements ready to be filled with delicate mosses their colours acting like a natural barometer of the English climate. All this was exciting. But not half as exciting as the weird panels in which the whole thing was to be sheathed, which were just starting to go up. Working in collaboration with artist Michael Craig-Martin – known for his vivid use of colour – Herzog and his partner Pierre de Meuron had decided to wrap the entire building in sheets of cheap polycarbonate, striped variously magenta, green and turquoise. The Laban Centre, their first completely new building in Britain, was going to look like a giant kaleidoscope.

Ask an architect to name the ten most famous practices at work today and you could safely wager that Herzog & de Meuron would feature. They might not top of the list – not yet, at least. California-based Frank Gehry, designer of the titanium-clad Guggenheim Museum in Bilbao, would probably score higher in terms of his international recognition. But then he is a generation older. Still only in their early 50s (that's just getting into your stride when it comes to architecture) Herzog & de Meuron's rise has been meteoric. Over the past 15 or so years they have established themselves as superstars in the design world with a string of astonishing buildings, their ceaselessly inventive architecture making even Gehry's writhing forms look somehow predictable and tame.

# H E R Z O G &

It is this ability to continually surprise – the constant reinvention of their style, their refreshing lack of preconceptions about what their buildings look like – that marks them out as some of today's most interesting designers. Most architects have a recognizable "house style"; when you hear that Gehry, Norman Foster or Daniel Libeskind (to name just a few of today's other superstar architects) is designing a new building you can have a fair idea of what it will look like. Not so with Herzog & de Meuron; you never know what they will come up with next.

**"NOTHING,"** "IS MORE boring OR stupid THAN TO WAKE UP IN THE MORNING **NAIVELY CONFIDENT** IN WHAT YOU ALREADY KNOW."

JACQUES HERZOG, TALKING TO JEFFREY KIPNIS

The day that they woke up and started on their competition-winning design for the Laban dance centre, Herzog & de Meuron put behind them the building that catapulted them to international fame – the conversion of London's Bankside power station into the Tate Modern gallery of art. Looked at together, you would be hard-pressed to know that the two buildings are by the same architects. At the Tate, Herzog & de Meuron took a minimal approach retaining much of the

# DE MEURON

existing building and simply adding a new two-storey "light box" to the roof – a glazed structure that provides views out across the capital and brings light down into the galleries.

As one of London's Millennium projects, the Tate predates by a couple of years the Laban Centre which is due to open its doors to dance students in autumn 2002. Architecture is a process of constant evolution, of course, and architects' styles develop over time; you wouldn't expect buildings designed two years apart from each other to be identical but the differences between the two are striking. That this is a feature of their work is illustrated by another Herzog & de Meuron building due to have been finished at much the same time as the Laban: the pair's Tokyo flagship store for fashion house Prada. Where the Laban is a low-slung two-storey building wrapped in sheets of cheap coloured plastic, Prada is a lantern-like tower made of faceted glass behind which a complex system of tube-shaped passages criss-cross their way up the shop's interior helping both to stiffen the building's structure and to add drama to an already spectacular building.

A determination never to do the same thing twice characterizes Herzog & de Meuron's growing body of work and yet, as we stride around the Laban's muddy building site and Jacques Herzog explains the ideas behind the project, a number of underlying themes become apparent – preoccupations that recur time and again, albeit expressed in different ways in all their buildings. Among others, these are a fascination with contemporary art and artists' ways of working, an interest in fashion and a desire to explore the possibilities offered by all sorts of building materials.

To get behind these interests and to see what drives them, we need to look, for a moment, at the firm's two founding partners – Jacques Herzog and Pierre de Meuron. They have known each since childhood when their parents sent them to the same Basle kindergarten. Firm friends ever since, they decided to become architects and both enrolled at the Eidgenössische Technische Hochschule (or ETH the Swiss technical University in Zürich) at a time when the school was a hot-bed of ideas (it is striking how many of today's now-famous Swiss architects were educated at the ETH). Studying architecture isn't just about learning how to design buildings that stay up, although this is vital; at its best architecture school is also a place where students learn to stretch their imagination and think creatively. Gottfried Semper, the ETH's nineteenth-century founder, claimed that "artistic production and the enjoyment of art requires a certain carnival spirit ... the carnival half-light is the true atmosphere of art."

On leaving the ETH, Herzog and de Meuron appear to have taken his advice quite literally. In 1978 they set up an office together in Basle. Their first project was a collaboration with the artist Joseph Beuys – the young architects persuaded him to help them design not a building but a suit to be worn by the 70 members of a marching band who paraded through the city centre. From the outset, then, collaborating with artists and an interest in fashion have underpinned their work. Herzog has a particular reason for being interested in clothes and how they are made as his mother was a tailor. "I am personally very attracted by clothes and textiles. My mother ... has always had all the textile stuff around her which attracted me a lot," he told the critic Jeffrey Kipnis (1). At one level, this is simply reflected in what they wear – Herzog (who is the practice's front man – de Meuron is much more retiring) is keen on sharply cut, slim-fitting clothes that accentuate his long, lean frame. At another level, fashion has profoundly influenced their architecture: "So many people think that contemporary fashion, music and even art are superficial when compared to the aspirations and responsibilities of architecture. But we disagree," Herzog explained. "These are practices that shape our sensibilities, they are expressions of our times. It is not the glamorous aspect of fashion which fascinates us. In fact we are more interested in what people are wearing, what they like to wrap around their bodies ... We are interested in that aspect of artificial skin which becomes so much of an intimate part of people."

If clothes are the outer layer in which we wrap our bodies and the way we present ourselves to the world, architecture's equivalent is the façade, the outside skin that sheathes the building. In Herzog & de Meuron's work the façade is the most significant element. The arrangement of the rooms inside is important too but never as important as the treatment of the façade which they accentuate in a range of different ways.

This interest in the surface layer is one they have in common with artists; in a number of

> "I AM PERSONALLY VERY **ATTRACTED** BY clothes AND textiles. MY **MOTHER** ... HAS ALWAYS HAD ALL THE **TEXTILE STUFF** AROUND HER WHICH ATTRACTED ME A LOT,"
>
> JACQUES HERZOG

their buildings they handle the façade just as an artist would – as a canvas to be decorated. Working with artists is also, like fashion, a way to engage with contemporary culture. "We prefer art to architecture, and for that matter artists to architects," Herzog says ([2]). From their initial collaboration with Beuys, Herzog & de Meuron has worked with a number of Europe's leading painters and photographers. It is not unheard of for architects and artists to collaborate, in fact it happens quite a bit – many countries give grants to artists or require clients to set aside a percentage of the building budget for art. But generally the art is an afterthought, a nice touch bolted on to the building at the end. Herzog & de Meuron's approach is different. Perhaps because of their long-standing friendship (Herzog says he and de Meuron have been a "partnership" since kindergarten), they are open to real collaboration with others. It is typical that at the Laban, Michael Craig-Martin was involved in developing the project from the start.

"WE prefer ART TO architecture, AND FOR THAT MATTER ARTISTS TO architects,"

JACQUES HERZOG

Perhaps it is no surprise that Herzog & de Meuron is caught up in the art world – Basle, where the practice is based, is one of the centres of the international art market. The Basle art fair is a key event in the contemporary art calendar, bringing together dealers representing most of today's top artists. In other ways too, being Swiss – and, particularly, coming from Basle – has helped shape the pair's outlook.

Switzerland may still like to sell itself to tourists as a land of cuckoo clocks, alpine chalets and cows with bells around their necks, but the idea of Switzerland as a rural backwater populated by the likes of Heidi and her mountain friend Peter is limited. The mountain communities and Alpine landscape of tourist brochures owe their continued existence to handsome subsidies granted them by cities such as Basle which generate huge wealth from banking and high-tech manufacturing. Don't be fooled by the city's picturesque setting on the banks of the river Rhine, its winding medieval streets, or its houses dating back to the fourteenth century; Basle is a thoroughly modern city and the centre of Switzerland's lucrative pharmaceuticals industry (the wealth from which helps finance the city's obsession with art). This is mirrored in Herzog & de Meuron's work, where an interest in industrial architecture is just as apparent as a love of traditional vernacular buildings. However, when looking at architecture of any style, it is to "anonymous buildings" that the pair is drawn, Herzog says, rather than flashy, important ones – an attitude informed in part perhaps by Basle's staunchly Protestant history.

The Dutch architect Rem Koolhaas (who has, on occasion, collaborated with the pair) believes geography accounts for much of the emotional impact of Herzog & de Meuron's work. "Part of their strength is that they are, in an inspiring way, 'in between' the north and the south, the unstable and the stable, the difficulty with being that haunts northern Europe, the oversimplification of being that limits the south ... you can see their work as a 'new life'," he wrote in an essay on their work (3). In a more direct way too, he believes the power of their work derives from a tension between opposites: "Those who know Jacques Herzog confront an explosive temperament rigidly controlled; in the work, the control is always evident, the explosive energies repressed, displaced ...[Herzog and de Meuron] are always correct, always serious, but at the same time with a suggestion of danger. Together their paradoxical abilities explain their success and critical popularity. Their work makes architecture again believable".

> **"YOU CAN SEE THEIR**
> **WORK** AS A
> **'new life',"**
>
> REM KOOLHAAS

Herzog and de Meuron's rise to the ranks of the world's most famous architects has been rapid but it did not happen over night. Like all architects – once they'd moved on from designing suits with Beuys, that is – they began with relatively small-scale buildings. For much of the 1980s they built houses and blocks of flats mostly in and around Basle. Even in early works, like the Stone House (1988), the Hebelstrasse apartment block (1988), or the Storage Building for cough sweet manufacturer Ricola (1991), you see a fascination with taking building materials and pushing them to new extremes whether it is traditional dry-stone walling (as with the house), timber construction (the apartment block), or industrially-produced cladding panels (the storage building) – a theme that has continued through all of their work.

The first building to receive significant critical acclaim was the gallery they designed for the Goetz Collection (1992). Set in a residential suburb of Munich, the site chosen for this private gallery of late twentieth-century art was hedged in by restrictions – the height of the cornice and the maximum size of each floor were dictated by local by-laws. Herzog & de Meuron's solution was to partially bury the two-storey building. Given this arrangement, the standard thing to do would have been to use the subterranean area to create dark rooms where video art and other pieces that need black-out conditions could have been viewed and to use the upper floor for pieces best seen in daylight. Instead, Herzog & de Meuron chose to reverse the arrangement: a frosted glass strip wraps around the building at ground level bringing light into the partially submerged lower level, above this is a windowless wider band of rendered birch plywood, and the whole thing is topped off by another glass clerestorey.

The result is an unsettling building. The sandwiched layers of glass and plywood suggest from the outside that the building will be three- not two-storeys tall – something truly anathema to modern architecture, which is thoroughly hung-up on the idea that the exterior of a building should "express" what is going on inside. More disturbing still is the way that the solid plywood panels appear to hover above the insubstantial glass base. There is nothing inherently unsafe about this (glass can be just as solid as wood), it is just that it feels unsafe – as though the glass plinth will not be able to support the rest of the building.

Quite a number of Herzog & de Meuron's early works have this quality of challenging the viewer. It is as if they are testing you; seeing how you react; making you rethink your ideas of what a building can be. The halls of residence they designed for the University of Burgundy in Dijon, France (1992) in collaboration with the Swiss artist Rémy Zaugg fall absolutely into this category of "difficult" buildings. Unremittingly featureless, save for small variations in the tone of the grey concrete they are constructed from, the 353 apartments are grouped in 300 metre (900 foot)-long blocks with deck-access stairs. The result is reminiscent of some 1960s social housing – and not the best of it, either.

None of their buildings since have been as unrelenting and, in fairness, the budget for the halls of residence did not allow for much else. All Herzog & de Meuron buildings bring you up short but usually it is with delight at their inventiveness, the delicate lightness of their touch. A good example of this is the second building they designed for Ricola, a production and storage building in Mulhouse, France (1993). This, too, is a utilitarian building: a warehouse with 8-metre (26-foot)-deep cantilevered overhangs along two sides that provide protection while goods are being loaded and unloaded from trucks. To help bring light into the building, Herzog & de Meuron clad these long sides in panels of translucent polycarbonate (the same material they would later use at the Laban dance centre). Polycarbonate is an ordinary, cheap material – the sort of thing you might well find in a factory building. "We like the idea of taking this material from the rack," Herzog explains, "and turning it into something beautiful." So they screen printed the panels with a leaf motif taken from a photograph by Karl Blossfeldt. Repeated again and again down the length of the building (like an Andy Warhol "repeat" picture) the image becomes abstracted, like a curtain or fresco that veils the building creating different effects according to the light levels.

This idea of printing the façade of the building, of treating it like a canvas, is one that Herzog & de Meuron has experimented with in different ways. At the Pfaffenholz sports centre (1993), on Basle's border with France, the concrete blocks from which the changing rooms are constructed is imprinted with a pattern that makes the walls look as if they are built of rock. Elsewhere similar games confusing surface and materials are at play: the sports hall itself is covered in glass panels screen printed with a photograph of the particleboard that is used behind the cladding as insulation in the building.

The influential Spanish critic Luis Fernández-Galiano believes Herzog & de Meuron have created many astonishing buildings and "at least two absolute masterpieces" (4). The first was built shortly after the Ricola factory and sports hall. Like its predecessors, it too is a relatively ordinary kind of building made extraordinary by Herzog & de Meuron's treatment. As part of a reorganization of the area surrounding Basle station, the Swiss railway company needed a signal box to house a new, highly complex points switching system. Signal boxes are not the most glamorous building types – the five-storey concrete box is full of machinery and equipment that needs to be kept in dark conditions – but from these unpromising requirements the architects created a truly striking building.

Herzog & de Meuron's signal box (1997) stands like a strong, silent giant in the scrappy urban landscape of railway sheds, train tracks and passing traffic. Because the building requires few windows, the team was able to wrap the concrete structure with thin bands of copper like a huge parcel so that the building looks like an outsize Faraday box or a gargantuan battery. Strictly speaking, of course, the copper strips serve absolutely no function other than as a decorative outer skin (except where they form sunscreens over the building's few windows). This disjuncture between inside and out, between the look of the building and its construction, is wholly out of keeping with the tenets of Modernism;

generations of architects have been brought up in strict adherence to the guiding principle that "form follows function". Not so, Herzog & de Meuron, for whom the surface of the building so often acts as a veil – a tantalizing, enticing gauze through which to glimpse, but not fully see, what's going on inside.

And yet it would be wrong to wax too romantic about their work; there is also a tough streak running through Herzog & de Meuron's architecture. There's an uncompromising bluntness to the underlying forms of many of their buildings and not all have this delicate outer wrapping. Take the studio they designed in Mulhouse, France in 1996 for the Rémy Zaugg (the artist with whom they had collaborated on their "toughest" project to date – the Dijon student housing). This is a really stern little building: a concrete bunker of a place where the only decoration are the (deliberate) stains in the concrete caused by the rainwater as it runs down one side of the studio. The Rudin House in Leymen, France (1997) is equally severe. The house looks like a child's drawing of a house; a building pared down to the absolute essentials of pitched roof, chimney, four walls, windows. There's not a hint of a frill, not a superfluous detail in sight. In fact, on first inspection, it looks so utterly minimal that it appears to have no front door – it takes a moment to figure out that the house is on a sloping site and you enter at basement level.

It is this tug of war between toughness and delicacy that gives Herzog & de Meuron's architecture its edge, its contrary allure. In some instances the two come together and this is when their buildings are at their very best. Their second "masterpiece" is just such a building: the Dominus winery (1998) in California's Napa valley.

The setting is spectacular: Christian Mouiex's vineyard runs along the bottom of a valley, its neat trellises of vines creating a seemingly never-ending grid that disappears into the distance until cultivated nature finally meets wilderness and the flat open landscape gives way to rolling hills. Herzog & de Meuron's winery for the French wine maker feels like part of the landscape. The long, low building sits at the centre of the site, aligned with the trellises of vines and bisected by the road that runs down the middle of the estate. Like the rows of vines that are kept in place by the carefully maintained system of posts and wires, the building is a piece of nature tamed. More than 90 metres (300ft) long, 25 metres (82 feet ) wide and 9 metres (30 feet) high, the whole thing is constructed from stone gabions – metal cages filled with loose rocks – a building technique more frequently used for heavy engineering projects than high-end architecture. The use of gabions is highly practical: it is a cheap way of building very thick walls and therefore a good way of insulating the winery against the extreme fluctuations in temperature between night and day. But as the light filters between the gaps in the stones, casting an ever-changing pattern across the inside of the building, it is obvious that the result is far more than just practical. Herzog describes the building as "very solid – almost archaic" and, in the next breath, as "lace-like". And he's right: it is robust and delicate at the same time, a man-made object inspired by nature, a building full of contradictions that somehow manage to pull together with incredible impact.

With the completion of the Dominus Winery, the world started to sit up and take note of Herzog & de Meuron's architecture. Their buildings are so intensely photogenic that they lend themselves to publication: the winery was snapped up not just by art and architecture magazines but also by the mainstream media – the building was seen in newspapers and colour supplements all overt the world. Despite the obvious appeal of the buildings on the page, their take up is surprising. Modern architecture isn't generally known for its widespread appeal and, given its often uncompromising starkness and its unfashionable earnestness ("we abhor cynicism" Herzog says), you'd be forgiven for thinking Herzog & de Meuron's architecture would not be popular. Yet it is. Perhaps it is the architects' very seriousness that appeals. As Terence Riley, head of architecture and design at the Museum of Modern Art in New York, suggests, perhaps the public feels that it is being taken seriously and responds accordingly.

"AT A TIME WHEN ALL human experience IS BEING CONVERTED TO A MODE OF **ENTERTAINMENT**, THEIR WORK RETAINS AN aura OF gravitas"

TERENCE RILEY

Of course, it is one thing for photographs of your buildings to appear in the pages of glossy magazines, it is quite another for your buildings to achieve real popular approval. The big test of Herzog & de Meuron's mass appeal came in 1994 when the office won an international competition to design a new branch of the Tate museum of art in London, beating entries by some of the world's most famous architects. This was their first major public project, their first commission for such a high-profile client, their first building in Britain (a country well-known for its antipathy towards contemporary design) and, not surprisingly, the team's progress was watched with considerable interest from all quarters.

As work began transforming a derelict power station on the south bank of the river Thames into a new gallery for the museum's world-class collection of twentieth (and, in due course, twenty-first) century art, a fly-on-the-wall TV documentary charted its development. Broadcast just before the gallery opened its doors in the summer of 2000, the series seemed to confirm the public's worst preconceptions about architects; endless arguments about costs were revealed, rows with the builders about the quality of the workmanship, and prima donna-ish behaviour by Jacques Herzog who would abruptly leave important meetings saying that he needed to go for a run. And yet the public took the building to its heart. On the first weekend alone, 90,000 visitors crowded into the refurbished turbine hall and made their way up zigzagging escalators to the new galleries and up again to the seventh floor where Herzog & de Meuron's new glass roof-top extension provided not just natural lighting for the galleries below but also some of the best views to be had across the London skyline. A real palace for the people, Londoners couldn't believe their luck: the chief criticism voiced was that the crowds made seeing the art virtually impossible.

Since the Tate, commissions have flooded in. The office remains in Basle and working methods continue much as they always have – the studio is littered with 1:1 mock-ups and models and, despite the addition of two new partners, Herzog and de Meuron still oversee all projects. But the number of staff has had to increase dramatically and the range of projects expanded. The practice still does some work in Basle, though. One of its most recently completed projects is a new stadium for Basle FC. As you would expect, it's no ordinary stadium. Herzog & de Meuron has covered the outside with hundreds of little cupolas (a cheap, acrylic off-the-shelf product) that, seen from a distance, give the impression the building is covered in bubble wrap. "Being so ordinary, materials become quite sexy – at least if you use them in the right way," Herzog explains. And he is right: at night you see through the semi-opaque bubbles to the red underside of the stadium – a deliberately vibrant red chosen to heighten the green of the pitch and as a nod to the team's colour. You could count on the fingers of one hand the number of football stadiums around the world that are as striking.

Few offices of the size that Herzog & de Meuron now is manage to maintain the inventiveness that characterizes its work. Perhaps this will change over time but at present there is no sign of it: the Laban Centre and Prada Tokyo both promise to be thoroughly provocative buildings and the string of new commissions coming up behind them look just as promising. True to their word, Jacques Herzog and Pierre de Meuron are still getting up in the morning and thinking anew about the world around them.

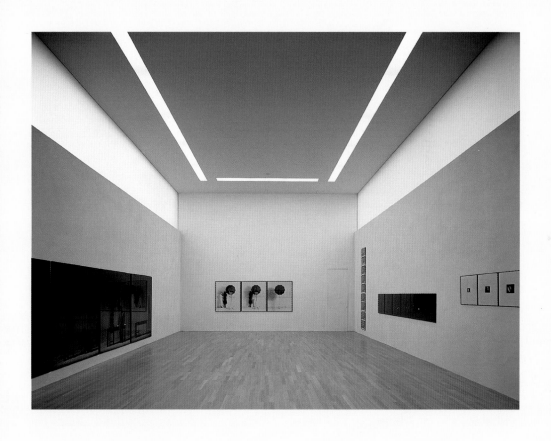

## FAME

Herzog & de Meuron's reputation grew rapidly during the 1990s. It was winning the international competition to design Tate Modern that firmly established it as one of today's leading architects' practices.

## MATERIALS

There are no rules as to what a Herzog & de Meuron building looks like. But – like the Dominus Winery in California – all use materials innovatively.

## ART HOUSE

Similarly, there is a tendency towards borrowing from the art world whether literally, as in the Blossfeldt motif (left) or more loosely.

## INSIDE OUT

The difference between interior and exterior spaces tends to blur in Herzog & de Meuron buildings. At the Ricola marketing building (1999) the outdoor space is roofed over with planting.

## INTERNATIONAL

Herzog & de Meuron now builds all over the world. Its apartment buildings in the rue des Suisses, Paris (2001), play all sorts of games with the notion of shutters.

## CONSISTENCY

Key themes – simple shapes and everyday materials – are already apparent in early works like the Blue House (left) the Studio Frei (top right) and Plywood House (bottom right).

## STONE HOUSE

The Stone house in Tavole, Italy (1988) took traditional dry stone walling techniques used in the area and gave them a very contemporary twist.

## STUDENT HOUSING, DIJON, FRANCE

The 355 apartments that Herzog & de Meuron designed on the University of Burgundy campus at Dijon, France (1992) are among their toughest buildings.

## GOETZ GALLERY

As unsettling but less brutal is the Goetz gallery (1992), in a Munich suburb, where glass and concrete combine in unusual ways.

## INSIDE GOETZ

The gallery is partially sunken, making it surprisingly big inside. The glass strips along top and bottom bring daylight deep into the heart of the building.

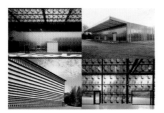

## RICOLA STORAGE BUILDING

Herzog & de Meuron clad the Ricola headquarters in Mulhouse, France (1993), in cheap polycarbonate panels which it printed with a Blossfeldt leaf motif.

## PFAFFENHOLZ SPORTS CENTRE

Again, printing techniques are used at the Pfaffenholz sports centre, St Louis, France (1993) to decorate the surface of the otherwise minimal building. Inside the centre is surprisingly light.

## APARTMENT BUILDING, BASLE

A 1993 apartment block designed in the practice's home town of Basle.

## ATELIER ZAUGG

Herzog & de Meuron likes to collaborate with artists. The firm has worked with Rémy Zaugg who returned the compliment, asking it to design him a studio in Mulhouse, France (1996).

## ATELIER ZAUGG

The studio is exceedingly simple: a concrete box with simple roof lights and oversailing roof. The only decoration is the (deliberate) way the rain stains the concrete walls.

## CARTOON MUSEUM/RUDIN HOUSE

Many Herzog & de Meuron projects have been tiny. The extension to the Cartoon Museum in Basle (left, 1996) measured 6 x 25 metres (20 x 80 feet). The Rudin house (1997) is, itself, like a small cartoon house.

### RUDIN HOUSE

The house in Leymen, France, is so minimal that it does not appear, at first sight, to have a front door; you enter from below.

### DOMINUS WINERY

The Dominus winery in California's Napa Valley (1997) is made from gabion walls – wire cages filled with stones – a technique borrowed from heavy engineering projects like the building of motorway verges.

### DOMINUS WINERY

The heavy gabion walls create a perfect thermal barrier to protect the wine-making process inside from the extreme fluctuations of heat outside.

### RICOLA MARKETING BUILDING

Herzog & de Meuron has designed three buildings for cough sweet manufacturer Ricola. This latest one in Laufen, Switzerland (1999) is designed with landscape architect Dieter Kienast.

### HOSPITAL PHARMACY, BASLE

The relationship between the skin of the building and its structure is emphasized by the Institute for Hospital Pharmaceuticals in Basle (1997). The whole thing is wrapped in an envelope of screenprinted glass.

## EBERSWALDE LIBRARY

Similarly, the exterior of the Eberswalde technical school library (1996), Germany, is treated like a single surface to be decorated – this time glass and concrete alike are printed.

## EBERSWALDE LIBRARY

The prints are photos that the German artist Thomas Ruff acquired over the years. They are screen printed onto the surface of the library.

## KUPPERSMUHLE

While working Bankside powerstation in London into Tate Modern, Herzog & de Meuron converted the Kuppersmuhle brickworks in Duisburg, Germany into a modern art museum (1999).

## SIGNAL BOX

One of Herzog & de Meuron's most iconic buildings is the signal box it designed in Basle (1997). The building is wrapped in fine bands of copper.

## APARTMENTS, MUNICH

The Five Courtyards project in Munich (2001) and the commercial and apartment building complex in Solothum.

## TATE MODERN

Herzog & de Meuron's transformation of a derelict power station into a new gallery for modern art (2000) was an instant hit with the visiting public which flocked to the gallery in their thousands.

## TATE MODERN

The architects kept the main turbine hall as a foyer, wrapping galleries around the Thames-side façade and adding a new "light box" to bring daylight into the spaces

## TATE MODERN

The architects' competition-winning scheme beat others by many of the world's most famous designers, helping to secure Herzog & de Meuron's international standing.

## APARTMENTS, RUE DES SUISSES, PARIS

The various apartment buildings in the rue des Suisses complex, Paris (2001) take on ideas of the skin. Here plants are encouraged to cover the building's surface.

## APARTMENTS, RUE DES SUISSES, PARIS

Elsewhere, shutters create a façade that can be changed at will by residents, depending on temperature and time of day. The project is a neat infill site off a busy main road

# Acknowledgements

All images courtsey Margherita Spiluttini (©copyright).
www.spiluttini.com

# Footnotes

1/2. Jeffrey Kipnis, "A Conversation [with Jacques Herzog]", El Croquis 1981–2000

Herzog & de Meuron

3. Rem Koolhaas, 'New Discipline', AV Monographs 77 May–June 1999

4. Luis Fernández-Galiano, 'H&dM, the first decades', AV Monographs 77 May–June 1999

5. Terence Riley, 'Gravitas and the media', AV Monographs 77 May–June 1999